CW00428750

SMILE!

A collection of whimsical poems

written and illustrated

by

AB Wyze

2021©

ISBN 9798545613120

abwyzestories@gmail.com

Published 2021
All content layout and design copyright© A B Wyze
All rights reserved. This book is sold to the condition
that it may not be reproduced, stored in a retrieval
system or transmitted in any form or by any means,
electronic, mechanical, photocopying, recording or
otherwise without prior consent of the author

Book
Five

CONTENTS

THE TORTOISE AND THE SNAIL

"I would not want to bore you,"
said tortoise to the snail,
"don't be afraid to tell me if I do.
It's just that you were yawning,"
he added with a frown,
"and I am nowhere near one-half way through."

"I'm sorry I was yawning,"
the snail said, open-mouthed.
"I haven't missed a word that you have said.
A fascinating subject,
I never would have thought
that you could talk for hours about a shed."

"A summerhouse," yelled tortoise.
"They built it just for me,
it's solid wood and very comfy too.
They clearly love me dearly,
I am their favourite pet.
They would not build a summerhouse for you!"

"I don't think I would want one."
the snail replied at once,
"I much prefer green cabbage for my bed.
It's lovely there at night time,
I munch and sleep and munch,
and you sir cannot surely eat a shed."

"A summerhouse!" yelled tortoise,
"a luxury chalet.
Your ears need washing out it now appears."
"I'd love to see you do it,"
the little snail replied,
"for snails, you see, do not have any ears."

"And yet sir," said the tortoise,
"you hear my every word,
you're telling little tales again that's true."
"It's not a lie," the snail said,
"it is a well-known fact,
I have no ears and neither sir do you.

Although you are a reptile
and I'm a gastropod
we surely are related you and me.
We both hear by vibrations
we pick up through our feet.
Quite clever that, I'm sure you will agree."

The tortoise started yawning
and looked down at the snail
"I s'pose you're right," is what the tortoise said.
"But hardly fascinating
or worthy of a speech...
let's talk about my summerhouse instead."

A TROLL WILL ONLY EAT YOU IF YOU'RE TASTY

A troll will only eat you
if you're tasty.
A troll won't touch you
if your skin is tough.
He'll give your skin a pinch,
and if it's tough, he'll flinch.
He'll say, "No thanks,
I've eaten quite enough."

But if you are a
tender looking morsel
and if your skin
is very soft and pink,
a troll will lick his lips
he'll serve you up with chips.
He'll eat you in the time
it takes to blink!

A troll won't eat your granddad
or your granny.
He'd rather chew
a sandal or a shoe.
But if you are a child
his eyes will just go wild!
Oh he would love
to sink his teeth in you!

So if you find yourself
down by the river,
and if you hear
some noises from a cave.
Do not investigate,
or it could be too late.
Oh it would be quite foolish
to be brave.

A troll could hide itself
inside some bushes.
A troll could hide behind
a nearby rock.
So if you hear a sound
and start to look around
you could be in for
one big nasty shock!

And you might think
those trolls are all slow witted,
but let me tell you sunshine,
they are not.
And they will drag you in,
and they will pinch your skin,
and if it's soft
they'll pop you in their pot!

SWEET SUCCESS

When I invented nougat sweets
that don't lock up your jaw,
those companies were not impressed
until I showed them more.

I showed them how this sweet of mine
did not make mouths clamp shut
despite its nougat content
and those gooey covered nuts.

The opposite was true
and conversation did not drop.
In fact, whoever chewed my sweet
began to talk non-stop.

Talk and talk with no respite
despite Nougat chew.
Those companies were now impressed
as this was something new.

I signed my name and bingo
we were in production fast,
a nougat bar that made you talk,
I'd made my name at last.

I floated on a cloud I did,
I wallowed in the fame,
but then the boardroom called on me
to come up with a name.

"Well I have that," I said to them,
"and I will give it TO you.
I will call my wonder bar…
the Chatter Nougat Chew Chew!"

SELF-ISOLATION

Me granny's in self-isolation,
me granny has locked herself in.
She says it's the Government's orders.
She's all locked away with the gin.

I heard her with nails and a hammer,
she's boarded the door from inside.
I asked her if I could get in there
she told me to 'go take a ride!'

Me granny's in self-isolation
and we have no clue what to do.
And nature ain't calling it's screaming...
she's locked herself up in the loo!

I WENT UP TO HEAVEN

I went up to heaven
and stood by the gate.
Some old bearded geezer
he asked me to wait.

He gave me some papers
and showed me a seat.
He said they were forms
which I had to complete.

I ticked loads of boxes
and signed on the line.
The old bearded geezer
he said it looked fine.

He gave me a number
I stood in a queue.
The number I had
was ten million and two.

He saw my face drop
and he gave me a grin
he said in ten years
I might be getting in.

I did not respond
and he started to laugh
he blamed it on paperwork;
shortness of staff.

I said, "That's no good
I have lived like a saint."
I said I would lodge
an official complaint.

He gave me a form
which he asked me to fill.
He showed me a chair
saying, "You know the drill."

I filled in the form
and I signed on the line.
The old bearded geezer
he said it looked fine.

He showed me a door
and he ushered me through
to stand at the back
of a twenty-mile queue.

And I have been queueing
for almost five years.
The old bearded geezer
he sometimes appears.

With forms in his hands
he just walks up the line
but nobody offers
to take one to sign.

I went up to Heaven
and stood by a gate.
A little bird tells me
I'm gonna be late!

CAT

The Cat sat on the floorboards;
we haven't got a mat.
But we do have a most disgruntled Cat.

THE WORLD OF SHIRLEY COOMBS

First of all I'd like to say
that Shirley is my friend.
Nothing more and nothing less
so let that be an end.

I'm a man of medicine
and though we share these rooms.
I'm a man, I'm my own man,
and so is Shirley Coombs.

Shirley is a genius,
unrivalled in his skill.
Solving the unsolvable,
he cracks those crimes at will.

He might seem peculiar,
all geniuses can.
But if you've a crime to solve
then Shirley is your man.

My name is Doctor Whatnot
but Shirley calls me What.
There is no doubt that I am
the best friend he has got.

Mrs. Hugsome runs this house
that sits on Butcher Street.
I don't trust her very much;
she isn't too discreet.

Copland Yard will call us up
with cases they can't crack.
They all know that Shirley Coombs
will get them back on track.

It is true enough to say
no week would be complete.
If there was no visit from
Inspector Paul Le Street.

Yesterday that man was here
sat in that very chair.
Pale as white asparagus,
and that was just his hair.

They had found a body in
a locked and sealed up room.
Everyone said suicide
but not so Shirley Coombs.

Pacing up and down the room
he made the copper wait.
Blowing bubbles from his pipe,
it helps him concentrate.

Shirley took the facts to mind,
and then screwed up his face.
After half an hour he cried
"Aha, I've cracked this case!"

"Oh Le Street," he shouted out,
"you've missed the clues again.
This was not a suicide,
allow me to explain.

Ask yourself," he muttered as,
he blew a bubble wide.
"why the dead man locked that door
and hid himself inside?"

"He preferred his privacy?"
Le Street asked with a grin.
Shirley blew a bubble, high,
then popped it with a pin.

"Privacy or secrecy?"
his whisper sounded dry.
"Next to him you found a box,
but did you wonder why?"

"Box was empty Shirley,"
said the man from Scotland Yard.
"Oh my word," said Shirley Coombs,
"You're making this so hard.

You described the room as dark,
the blinds were closed up tight.
You said when you all broke in
it was as dark as night.

But the box lay empty, ah,
but did you care? Oh no.
It was what was in that box
that dealt the fatal blow.

Find a man whose travels have
been out to the far east.
Search his rooms and you will find
a small yet deadly beast."

Well Le Street found such a man
and searched about his place.
Sadly one poor constable
was bitten in the face.

They secured the Ribbon Snake,
the man confessed right there.
Shirley filled his pipe bowl up
and bubbles filled the air............

HOW I GOT DETENTION

Our teacher brought a parrot in,
he set it on a chair.
He said its name was Polly
and the bird gave us a stare.

He said the parrot knew more things
than anyone in class.
He said that if he gave a test,
the parrot? It would pass.

And then he said the big green bird
was once a pirate's pet.
A pirate who had seen the world
from Boston to Tibet.

And then he walked up to the map
that we had in our room.
He pointed at a place on it...
the parrot said, "Khartoum!"

"And seven nines?" our teacher asked
the bird said "sixty-three."
"And eight times six?" I turned pure white
as he was asking me.

"Oh eight times six is forty-eight,"
the parrot duly squawked.
"And England's famous Dover cliffs
they constitute of chalk.

And Davy Crockett lost his life
inside the Alamo.
And if a cloud gets pushed too high
the rain will fall as snow."

And then the parrot rolled its eyes
and made a tutting sound.
Our teacher took the parrot's cage
and carried it around.

"This bird," he said, "will come to class
on every single day.
And you will all be grateful
for whatever it might say."

The parrot prattled on and on,
our teacher had a rest.
It talked about the stock market
and how we could invest.

It had a high-pitched whining voice
that pierced into our brains.
It talked about the pyramids
and mummified remains.

Our teacher just went off to sleep
the parrot whined away...
On how to make a building brick
with water and with clay.

The parrot squawked and talked and squawked
it drove us all quite mad.
Incessantly reminding us
of what a brain it had.

Then at the bell, our teacher woke
and gave the cage a stare.
The door to it was open wide...
the parrot was not there.

"No one leaves," our teacher screamed,
"until you let me know.
whichever one of you in here
has let my parrot go."

So sheepishly I raised my hand
and said, "Sir, it was me.
The parrot asked us what we knew
about geometry

I opened up the parrot's cage
so he could fly a while.
I told him that geometry
was really just my style.

I opened up the window then,
my thinking cap was on.
And, as it flew out of the room
I shouted...POLYGON!"

THE CONTINUING STORY OF JACK AND JILL

So, Jack and Jill got married,
they rang the Chapel bell.
The bridesmaids were Miss Muffet
and Pussy from the well.

The best man, Humpty Dumpty,
he made a rousing speech.
They honeymooned in Cornwall,
and frolicked on the beach.

They sailed into the sunset
a HUGE wave sank their boat.
And that's where they met Jonah
inside the Blue Whales' throat.

Above them on the surface,
upon the raging sea,
sailing in a whaling boat
were Tweedles… Dum and Dee.

And when the Blue Whale surfaced
their harpoon landed true.
They took the massive carcass
and cut it clean in two.

A monstrous Crow flew over
to scoop up Jack and Jill.
It carried them to Cornwall
and dropped them o'er a hill.

The two of them sent spinning
until they hit the ground,
they rolled across a hilltop
and then they tumbled down.

The Duke of York he found them,
and took them into town
where Doctor Foster cured them
with paper, coloured brown.

Oh, Jack and Jill had children,
they called them Jill and Jack,
They set up home in Holland
and never once looked back.

WHY YOU SHOULD NEVER STARE AT AN ATLAS

How arrogant the British,
for calling Britain Great.
And why don't other countries
do the same?

Why don't they shout out loudly
how wonderful they are?
There's nothing wrong
with making such a claim.

Like Mighty Madagascar
or Super-Duper Spain.
They have a ring
I'm sure you all agree.

Amazing Argentina
or Unique USA
and how about
Important Italy?

And then I got to thinking,
about some other things.
New Zealand seemed
to stick inside my head.

What happened to Old Zealand?
That's what I want to know.
And are the folk that lived there
now all dead?

And then of course there's Turkey,
who gave that place it's name?
They must have done
get some kicks.

Cause if they'd called it Chicken,
the Turks might be quite mad.
For they would not be Turks...
they would be Chicks.

THE WEASEL

"Us Weasels," said the Weasel,
"are just misunderstood.
We always play the bad guy,
we're never shown as good.
The Hedgehogs and the Rabbits,
the Squirrels and the Mice,
they're all portrayed as heroes,
it isn't very nice.
You illustrators draw them
as sweetly as you can.
But Weasels all look shady,
as if they'd rob your Gran.
We're all misrepresented;
we're cute for Heaven's sake.
So draw some pretty Weasels,
and give us guys a break!

THE GENTLE SEA

How kind the sea is
to allow us this playground,
to move back politely
without being asked.
To dampen the sand so perfectly
for our castles and dreams.
How understanding,
to wait within reach
like an obedient servant,
just in case we need to cool our feet,
splash like flounders or swim like bream.
How generous the sea
to lend us her treasures,
scatter them freely
across her wide beaches
without even asking that they be returned.

How kind the sea is.

IDENTICAL

Oh Magdelaine and Madeline
were evil witches to the core.
Though both of them loved children
they would NEVER EVER eat one raw.

That Magdelaine she much preferred
to have her children barbecued.
And Madeline she liked hers stewed
she did not care for smoky food.

The two of them
were very tall
and both of them
were very thin.
The two of them
had noses, hooked,
and each of them
had bright green skin.
The two of them
wore long black gowns
and both of them
wore pointed hats.
The two of them
rode spindly brooms
and each of them
owned fat black cats.

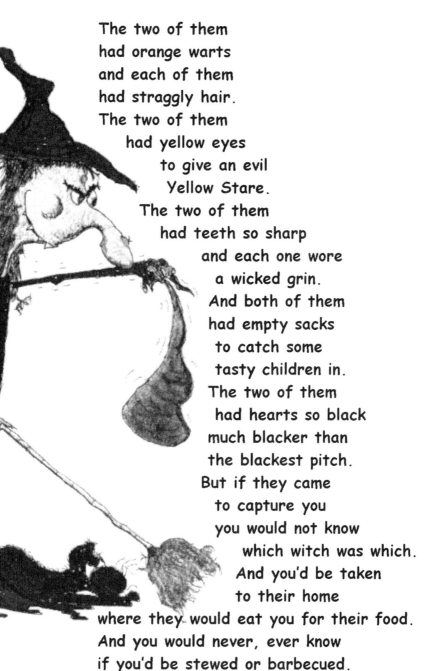

The two of them
had orange warts
and each of them
had straggly hair.
The two of them
   had yellow eyes
      to give an evil
         Yellow Stare.
   The two of them
      had teeth so sharp
         and each one wore
            a wicked grin.
            And both of them
            had empty sacks
               to catch some
               tasty children in.
            The two of them
               had hearts so black
            much blacker than
            the blackest pitch.
         But if they came
            to capture you
            you would not know
               which witch was which.
               And you'd be taken
               to their home
where they would eat you for their food.
And you would never, ever know
if you'd be stewed or barbecued.

CHICKEN DUMPLING STEW

My granddad's an explorer
he's travelled everywhere.
From Washington to Moscow,
Japan to Delaware.

And granddad's been to Asia
amongst the mountain peaks.
That's where he met the yetis
and stayed with them for weeks.

The Yetis ate spaghetti
it was their favourite dish.
They warmed it through with Yak's milk
and stirred in salted fish.

I haven't met those Yetis
but if I ever do.
I'll bring them back to England
for chicken dumpling stew.

All bubbling up with gravy
and dumplings crisp and hot.
Those Yetis they will taste it
and then they'll eat the lot.

Those Yetis love a snowfall
that's what my granddad said.
I'll bring them here in winter
we'll play out on my sled.

And I will be the best friend
that they have ever had.
I'll take them on a journey
and visit my granddad.

We'll do some snowball fighting.
They'll hit me on the chin.
But though I'd likely beat them
I might just let them win.

And then we'll get to granddads'
we'll hear that dinner bell.
We'll walk into the kitchen
and smell that cooking smell.

With stew upon the menu
the best that you can get.
Those yetis will tell stories,
they'll talk about Tibet.

They'll talk about the mountains
and avalanches too.
But they will all be thinking
of chicken dumpling stew.

They'll stay with us forever.
At weekends we will play
and they'll have chicken dumplings
on every single day.

THE MEREST SNIP

I'm not gonna tell ya how hard it all is
you've had pain, I know, and it hurts.
I'm not gonna cry or complain about this
cause I know that you've been through worse.

But everything baby is dragging me down
and pain is so hard to endure.
I hear what you're saying, I'm sure you mean well
but lately I aint been so sure.

Your smile is too perfect
Your eyes are so blue
But men have to do
what them men have to do.
Don't let me face this thing alone.

You tell me to grow up and act like a man,
you tell me that I should be tough.
Our love life's on hold and your pleading with me,
"Ain't seventeen children enough?"

But each of those children that I've given you
are testament to our deep love.
And now I feel like I am paying a price
an order from somewhere above.

His smile is too perfect
his eyes are too blue
but surgeons will do
what those surgeons will do.
Don't let me face this thing alone.

All women were born to bear children my love,
not my fault that I am a man.
But needles are needles and scalpels are sharp,
I'm fast going off your new plan.

All men-folk were born to give children my love,
there should be a law against this.
So what if we end up with twenty odd kids,
oh please let me give this a miss.

My smile has just vanished
my eyes must look rough.
They gave me a local,
that cain't be enough.
His knifes' getting close to the bone...

Don't let me face this thing alone.

CAMP VAMPIRE

The Vampire wore the Holy cross
and ate his garlic bread.
He'd done the same for countless years,
as he was well undead.

The Vampire dressed in powder pink,
his lips were painted red.
His siblings were out biting necks
of maidens in their beds.

The Vampire stood to check his hair,
then minced across the room.
One hand on hip, and one wrist limp.
They'd all be back quite soon.

The Vampire pulled the cooler door
and took a carton out.
He poured the blood into a glass,
his lips began to pout.

Reaching for the vodka then
he added just a shot.
He loved his Bloody Mary,
oh it really hit the spot.

And then the window opened and
his siblings all flew in.
The Vampire turned towards them
and he gave a crooked grin.

"I hope you wiped your feet" he said;
"I've only just cleaned through.
A woman's work is never done,
with no great help from you."

The siblings snarled and bared their teeth
The Vampire's grin was wide.
"And hang your cloaks up in the hall,
and leave those boots outside."

His eldest brother's hand reached out
to grab him by the head.
The Vampire flashed his Holy cross
and waved his garlic bread.

The siblings all removed their boots
and then removed their cloaks.
Then off they went into the hall
and not one sibling spoke.

The Vampire closed the window tight
and pulled the curtains too.
"I'll be so glad when morning comes,
I have so much to do."

I can't abide the biting stuff
and maidens turn me cold.
It's much too late for me to change,
I'm now six centuries old."

He gazed into his mirror to
put powder on a wart.
"And THEY have no reflection,
Oh, I shudder at the thought."

OH HELL!

I've only just arrived down here
it seems ok you know.
I'm sure that smell will dissipate
in just a day or so.

Yes Hell's a fine old place to be
in fact it's nice as Hell.
They serve you whiskey in your tea
and chocolate cake as well.

We may be standing knee deep in
a room of horse manure.
But I can tell you I have been
in worse than this before.

Oh now the Devil's just popped in
I don't like what he said.
"Tea break over now me lads
so, stand back on your heads."

HE JUMPED INTO PUDDLES

He jumped into puddles
the silly young fool.
He jumped into puddles
while going to school.

He splished and he sploshed
and he drenched passers-by.
He never said sorry
and never said why.

From children to parents
to much older folk.
Oh, even the reverend
got a good soak.

He splished and he sploshed
and he splashed low and high
and even umbrellas
could keep no one dry.

He jumped into puddles,
again and again.
The last one he jumped in...
well...
it was a drain.

I BOUGHT MYSELF A DONKEY

I bought myself a donkey
I bought it yesterday.
I fed him, gave him water,
supplied a bed of hay.
And everything was perfect,
except he didn't bray.

I gave him prods and pinched him,
no nearer did I get.
I stroked him and I poked him;
provoked my brand-new pet.
When nothing worked I told him,
"I'll take you to the vet."

The stethoscope the vet used
was pressed on donkey's chest.
But first he kindly warmed it
cos warming it was best.
He didn't lift his clothing
cos donkeys don't wear vests.

"Oh, dearie me," he mumbled
and then he said "of course."
He sat down and he whispered,
his head hung with remorse.
"You donkey's not a donkey,
your donkey is a horse!"

My horse came back to my place,
I rode it all the way.
I fed him, gave him water
supplied a bed of hay.
Oh, everything was perfect,
except it didn't neigh.

I pricked him and I kicked him,
no nearer did I get.
I squeezed and almost choked him.
I soaked my equine pet.
But then I had to tell him,
"I'll try a different vet."

This vet said "Leave him with me;
I'll sort it out somehow
for I've got all the potions
the Governments allow."
But very soon he told me,
"Your horse sir is a cow!"

The cow came back to my place,
I knew just what to do.
I gave her milk and water
and cud on which to chew.
Oh, everything was perfect,
except she did not moo!

I taunted and I teased her,
I pulled upon her tail.
I stood her up, I knelt her,
I hung her on a nail.
I played my banjo to her,
but that was bound to fail.

"The vets round here are useless,"
I whispered in her ear.
"I'll take you to my father,
he lives quite close to here.
And he'll soon have you mooing,
of that I have no fear."

Dad took her to his stable,
and then I heard her moo.
It shook the floor and ceiling,
it shook the windows too.
I sang and danced and shouted,
"I knew it I just knew!

But then there was a silence,
no sound did my cow make.
My dad came out to tell me
some news he had to break.
"Your cow is not a cow, lad,
your cow is now prime steak!"

JUST FOR KICKS

Nothing kicks as hard
as a Cassowary can,
It's the hardest kicking bird
ever known to man.
It could kick an Eskimo
half way to Japan...
no, nothing kicks as hard
as a Cassowary can.

I knew an explorer
oh, the poor unlucky chap.
A Cassowary kicked him hard,
it kicked him off the map.
He shot up into outer space,
way out amongst the stars.
So far, it's said he's now become
a satellite of Mars.

Nothing kicks as hard
as a Cassowary can,
It's the hardest kicking bird
ever known to man.
It could kick a Kangaroo
from Sydney to Oban...
no, nothing kicks as hard
as a Cassowary can.

A politician spouted out
these badly mistimed words,
"We must rid our planet
of the Cassowary Bird."
The Cassowary kicked him hard
from April into June.
And he now makes his speeches
from some place upon the Moon.

Nothing kicks as hard
as a Cassowary can,
It's the hardest kicking bird
ever known to man.
It kicked a naughty boy so hard
he landed as a man!
No nothing kicks as hard
as a Cassowary can.

So if the Cassowary
detects you on its trail,
prepare yourself beforehand
and pad up like a whale.
Don't bother writing home at all
to tell us you have failed,
chances are you'll be back home,
three days before the mail.

No, nothing kicks as hard
as a Cassowary can.
It's the hardest kicking bird
ever known to man.
If you want to travel
the cheapest way you can,
remember!

Nothing kicks as hard as a Cassowary can.

BORN WITH A RUNCIBLE SPOON

I was born with a runcible
spoon in my mouth
and a sharp, vorpal sword by my side.
When I opened the book
and the journey began,
I was kidnapped it can't be denied.

The owl and the pussycat
they are to blame,
for they bundled me into their boat.
The owl started singing
to that small guitar
and the pussycat swooned at each note.

The walrus and carpenter
waved from the shore
and we joined them for oysters that day.
The pen in my hand
had a life of its own
as I frantically scribbled away.

A whuffling and burbling
was heard from the wood
as the jabberwock managed a kill.
A smile with no face
that belonged to a cat
chased a turkey who lived on a hill.

Well, the Walrus just laughed
as the carpenter cried
and his tears turned to salt in the air.
We were joined in our feast
by a man known as Milne;
a boy and a book and a Bear.

And I woke the next night
with a smile on my face
and a head full of crazy ideas.
The Owl and the Pussycat
must take the blame
I've been stuck in their boat now for years.

PORCUPINE

A hedgehog is a friendly chap
despite his spiny skin.

A hedgehog has the sweetest face,
he has the cutest grin.

So if you meet a hedgehog
you should give your best to him.

A porcupine can shoot his spines
a porcupine's no fun.

Those porcupines are hard to find
but if you see one...run!

A porcupine is rather like...

a hedgehog with a

GUN!

GRANNY'S KNITTING

My granny is constantly knitting,
my gramp says that she never stops.
She knits while she's watching the TV,
she knits as they drive to the shops.

But gramp doesn't mind granny knitting,
he's glad that he made her his wife.
He says there have been odd occasions,
her knitting has saved someone's life.

He said they were out on safari.
In Africa, miles out of town.
They drove into wild lion country;
the jeep they were driving broke down.

They called up the nearest gamekeeper,
he said he'd be there in a bit.
My gramp he just started to panic,
my granny she started to knit!

For up on the hazy horizon,
about half a mile from their jeep.
A lion stood up from some grassland,
and stretched after taking a sleep.

It then started strolling towards them,
it quickly broke into a trot.
My gramp once again was in panic,
but thankfully granny was not!

She knitted much faster than ever,
and gramp was just frozen with fear.
His eyes they were fixed on the lion,
which was so uncomfortably near.

He then saw the red helicopter,
but gramp was expecting the worst.
The chopper would reach them, but surely,
the lion would get to them first.

Then granny stood up with her knitting,
and cast off the thing she had made.
And gramp said he knew in an instant,
his wife simply was not afraid.

She threw out her woolly creation,
and then told my gramp to relax.
It landed in front of the lion,
which simply stopped dead in its tracks.

It stared at what granny had knitted,
and gave it a grin really wide.
A net from the red helicopter,
trapped knitting and lion inside.

So yes, it was my granny's knitting,
that rescued them both from that mess.
She'd used all her skill with the needles
to knit up a cute lioness!

DAYDREAMING

If badgers kept budgies as pets
in cages all made out of nets
then fed them on grubs
and newly grown shrubs,
how different would those budgies get?
If badgers kept budgies as pets?

If all of our blackbirds turned blue
those experts would not have a clue.
It might make Bill Oddie
as useful as Noddy
and no one would know what to do.
If all of our blackbirds turned blue.

If man eating sharks sprouted wings
it would be a frightening thing.
They'd land on your shed
they'd bite off your head.
Just think of the panic they'd bring.
If man eating sharks sprouted wings.

If spiders were seven feet high
with webs that stretched up to the sky
just how will you feel
when they hunt for meals?
'Cause they won't be searching for flies.
If spiders were seven feet high.

If teachers all dressed up like clowns
and hung from the beams upside down.
You'd not feel a fool
when sitting in school.
You'd never be wearing a frown...
If teachers all dressed up like clowns.

If daydreaming got taught in school
I think it would be really cool.
I'm sure that I'd pass,
be top of the class.
I think they should make it a rule
that daydreaming gets taught in school.

FISH IN BATTER

Chitter chatter fish in batter,
chips and mushy peas.
Seaside walking, seagulls squawking
paddle to your knees.

Gulls are swooping, loop the looping
such a hungry brood.
They're insistent, most persistent
now they've seen your food.

Start to swelter there's no shelter
not one place to run.
Seagulls walking, seagulls stalking
out there in the sun.

Tastes are changing, rearranging
seagulls have one wish.
No more diving for surviving
when there's battered fish.

Chitter chatter fish in batter
mushy peas and chips.
It was costly but it mostly
never passed your lips.

POOR OLD FATHER POSTLETHWAITE

Poor old Father Popplethwaite,
overworked and underweight,
toured his Parish daily, like...
on his penny farthing bike.
Preaching here and preaching there,
preaching bloody EVERYWHERE!
Shouting from his saddle high
that the Judgement Day was nigh.
Did not see the village lake,
penny farthings have no brakes.
People tried but got there late...
poor old Father Popplethwaite.

Poor old father Popplethwaite
standing there at Heaven's gate,
tangled up with bits of bike...
from his mouth there hangs a Pike.
He is dazed and he's confused,
Peter has some real bad news.
"You tried much too hard," he claims,
"gave the church a real bad name.
You turned many folk away...
now for that sir you must pay.
Not for YOU the Pearly Gates..."
poor old Father Popplethwaite.

Poor old Father Popplethwaite,
he is in a right old state.
He thought he had been so good,
bible punching like he should.
He still has his rusty steed,
cycles round at no great speed.
On a bike that has no seat
in the burning Hades heat.
Preaching here and preaching there
preaching bloody everywhere!
Even though that sealed his fate...
poor old Father Popplethwaite.

MY DISNEY DAZE

Mickey Mouse and Minnie Mouse
what were they all about?
There was more to that affair
than Disney dare let out.

I suspected something though
and had to see it through.
Caught a plane to Disneyland
and took my camera too.

Goofy likes a little drink
it was not hard to see
Bleary eyes all puffed and red
he soon latched on to me.

I knew he could tell me more
of Mickey Mouse you see
All I had to do was shout
"The drinks are all on me."

In the bar that superstar
accepted all my drinks
talked about himself a lot
my heart began to sink.

All that guy could talk about
was his apparent fame
Did not take me long to see
how Goofy got his name...

Pluto ah, now there's a guy
who doesn't drink or smoke.
If you want a role model
then Pluto is the bloke.

Found him down the gym I did
yes, working on his pecs.
Getting eyed from far and wide
by all the fairer sex.

Pluto though was too involved
and he ignored their stares,
pumping iron and pushing weights
he was so unaware.

Playing to his vanity
I got an interview.
Went back to his private yacht
to share a grape or two.

Did I say Grape? Oh silly me
I said it out of hope.
Pluto slipped his speedos off
and then gave ME a grope.

He was stronger than a bull
and I was easy meat.
Then we heard up on the deck
the sound of slapping feet.

Donald Duck a charming gent
just in the nick of time,
came in through the cabin door
he carried beer and wine.

Tore a strip or maybe two
off that weird Pluto guy.
Led me back up to the deck
and then he winked an eye.

"Pluto thinks that any fan
will be at least fair game.
If you breathe a word of this
then you'll be sad you came."

Then the Duck, with some good luck
he took me to his house,
where he talked and talked and talked
of Mr. Mickey Mouse.

"I know things," he said to me,
"they're things that will appal.
If you'll get me out of here
then I will tell you all."

Then the door it fell right in
it crashed down to the floor.
And we saw old Goofy there
a lying on that door.

"Hold the fort," old Goofy wheezed,
he sounded rather hoarse.
"Minnie Mouse and Mickey Mouse
are filing for divorce."

Donald Duck put down his glass
and bowed his yellow head.
"If that's true," he duly groaned,
"then Disneyland is dead."

Making my excuses I
retreated from the room.
Only to be thwarted as
I tripped up on a broom.

Mickey Mouse himself appeared
his face it looked so pale.
As he shook my offered hand
he took away my ale.

"Minnie Mouse," said Mickey Mouse;
"has left me for some goon.
Gone to start a new career
with Bugs at Looney Tunes."

Donald Duck he gasped out loud
then Goofy just passed out.
All that booze and now this news
had got to him no doubt.

Mickey Mouse he drained MY glass
then gave it back to me.
"Fill her up," he duly squeaked,
"and I don't mean with tea."

I looked back at Donald Duck
the yellow one just shrugged.
"Im alone!" wailed Mickey Mouse
"I need a good strong hug...

Someone hug me NOW" he said,
then wished at once he'd not.
Pluto stepped into the room
and said, "Oh Mick; you're hot!"

Donald Duck and Mickey Mouse
that Pluto guy and me
we all sat round the mini bar
and sank a glass or three.

Goofy had a couple too
he drank them through a straw.
Pluto stuck it in his mouth as
he lay on the floor.

Then to everyone's surprise
Bugs Bunny sauntered in.
We all saw the lipstick stains
all spread around his chin.

"What's up Doc?" the Bunny said
and then he gave a laugh.
Taking out a carrot which
he promptly bit in half.

"Home destroyer!" Donald yelled,
"you have no feelings bud.
Why have you come round here now...
you after Mickey's blood?"

"Hold your horses Duck my friend,"
the chomping Bunny cried.
"It was she who went for me
I came in here to hide...

Boy that mouse she ain't no mouse
that gal is rabbit mad.
She's heard all the stories guys
and all of them are bad."

Just before his words got out
they all turned round to see
Minnie Mouse stood at the door
as pretty as could be.

"Scuse me stud," she simpered
as she brushed old Bugs aside.
"I came here to get my man,"
and Mickey blushed with pride.

"Don't know what I saw in you,"
she gave old Bugs a stare.
"Floppy ears and big buck teeth
and coarse, untidy hair."

Donald Duck he heaved a sigh
of unreserved relief.
Bugs had gone a might cross eyed
he looked down at his teeth.

Mickey Mouse and Minnie Mouse
went to the room next door.
Pluto eyed the Bunny up
and Goofy gave a snore.

Donald Duck then turned to me
and gave a little wink.
"No need now for me to leave
I'll stay right here I think."

I checked out of Disneyland
and caught the desert train.
I don't think I'll ever go
to that odd place again.

Desert trains they never stop
there are no stations there.
I lay back and closed my eyes
to dream of hope somewhere.

Then the train it stopped it did
oh miles from anywhere.
I was snoring peacefully
and I was unaware.

Then a noise alerted me
I sat up from my sleep.
I heard a wild coyote howl,
a roadrunner went BEEP!

THE BOGEYMAN

The Bogeyman won't come tonight,
he doesn't live round here.
He lives where the mountains are
and forests full of fear.
The Bogeyman he cannot fly
he does not have a car
so he'll stay in that mountain place
my house is much too far.
The Bogeyman could know someone
somebody he could call.
No, he is far too frightening
he has no friends at all..
The Bogeyman might catch a bus
there's loads of them round there.
No, he doesn't have a job
and can't afford the fare.
The Bogeyman might jump upon
the roof of some fast train.
No he won't; too dangerous
he could end up in pain.
The Bogeyman won't come tonight
it's much too far this place.
I'll turn the light out...
Turn it on...
I'd better... just in case.

THE LAST WORD

"Mr Knight," said the bishop,
"I have to object,
your attitude stinks sir,
you show no respect.

This is not a game
that we play on this board
and folk such as you
we can all ill afford.

You're flippant you're flighty
and that is not all,
one wrong move from you
and our King could well fall."

The rook in the corner
he nodded his head,
as if in agreement
with what had been said.

"Those knights think they're special,
they give me the hump.
It's only because
they can all flippin' jump!

A battle might rage
and then run its full course
but won't be resolved
by a man on a horse."

"Oh Bishop, oh Rook,"
said the knight on his steed,
"your views of a battle
are narrow indeed.

Yes I am flamboyant
and take the odd chance,
but I'm also deadly
with sword and with lance.

I stand on the white squares
and cover the black,
in solid defence
or in all-out attack.

You have to agree
there is no finer sight
than the leap and the thrust
of a gallant young Knight.

"There what did I say?"
said the rook with disdain.
"He's bragging about
all his leaping again.

Does he ever consider
or ever give thanks
to the trustworthy rook
who controls from the flanks?"

The battle worn bishop
he nodded his head,
as if in agreement
with all the rook said.

Another voice spoke
and the three of them froze
from the hairs on their heads
to the nails on their toes.

And they silently turned
and each one bowed his head,
the Queen had been listening
to all that was said.

"Oh you all have your uses,"
Her Majesty cried,
"from the pawns at the front
to the rooks down the side.

You have cut you have thrust
you have grit you have guile,
but you're no match for me!"
she put in with a smile.

"For I am the best
it cannot be ignored
as there is no square
I can't use on this board.

In defence or attack
I've been put to the test
and time after time
I've been proved to be best.

Now I give you the order
to bicker no more
and save all that angst
for the very next war!"

The Queen went to sleep
and so gently she snored,
she had had the last word
on that black and white board.

And no one complained,
such a thought was absurd,
but that word from the queen
it was not the last word...

The rook and the bishop
they rested a while,
the knight rested with them
but he wore a smile.

All three of them knew
that the queen had been right.
"But she still cannot jump,"
said the cheeky young knight.

AUTHOR'S NOTE

I do hope that you enjoyed this book, the fifth in a series of who knows how many. If you happen to be browsing and turned to this page first, I most sincererly suggest that you read at least three random poems before you decide whether to buy it or, indeed, steal it. I do not endorse the second option but let's face it, it happens.

As with the previous books in this series, I doubt that you will find a collection of poems covering such diverse subjects anywhere else. I am also confident that you would be hard pushed to come across a more entertaining anthology of poetry books. I pride myself on my diversity and upon my imagination when it comes to telling a whimsical tale in rhyme.

Please, if you did enjoy this book, spread the word, as I have this dream of world-domination so far as the humorous rhyming word is concerned. If you did buy the book, I thank you with all my heart. If it was a gift I urge you to drop very heavy hints in order that you receive more.

Thanks

Printed in Great Britain
by Amazon

65141681R00051